Faith Images: Clip Art for the Liturgical Year

Designs by
Placid Stuckenschneider, O.S.B.

Sheed & Ward

Published by Sheed & Ward, P.O. Box 419492, Kansas City, MO 64141-6492.
To order, call 1-800-333-7373.

Printed in the United States of America
ISBN: 1-55612-611-5

Contents

PREPARE THE WAY OF THE Lord

LORD SHALL COME

await HIS coming joyfully

Now the Lord is nigh!

Come, let us adore

A Blessed Christmas

COME,
LORD JESUS,
COME

A CHILD
IS BORN
TO US
THIS DAY

Rejoice IN THE LORD ALWAYS AGAIN I SAY

Rejoice THE LORD IS NEAR

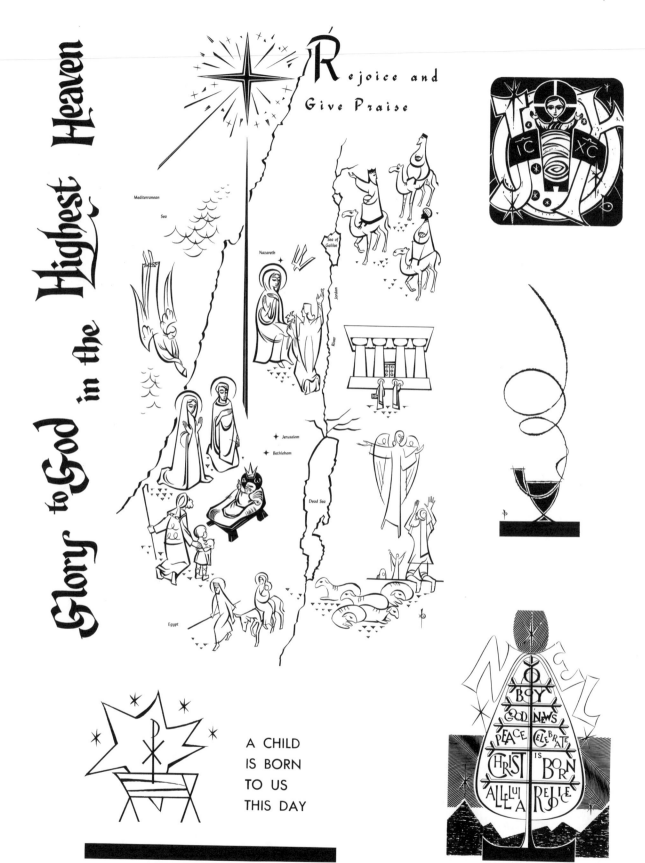

Glory to God in the Highest Heaven

Rejoice and Give Praise

A CHILD
IS BORN
TO US
THIS DAY

We have come from the East to worship the king.

Glory to God in the Highest Heaven

CHRIST IS BORN TO US,
COME, LET US ADORE

CHRIST IS BORN TO US.
COME. LET US ADORE

GLORY   glory   GLORY

glory

GLORY

GLORY

THEY SAW HIS STAR AND FOLLOWED IT

LENT · PRAYER · FAST

SPIRIT-RE-NEWAL · PENANCE

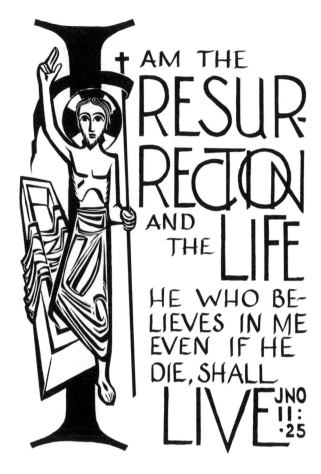

✝ I AM THE RESUR-RECTION AND THE LIFE HE WHO BE-LIEVES IN ME EVEN IF HE DIE, SHALL LIVE JNO 11:·25

I do not wish the sinner to die, says the Lord, but to turn to me and live.

FAST AND LAMENT BEFORE THE LORD

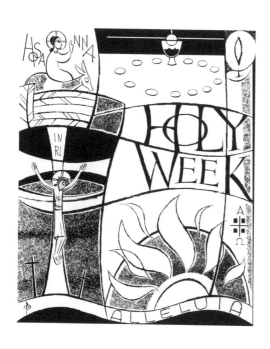

ALLELUIA CHRIST HAVING RISEN FROM THE DEAD, DIES NOW NO MORE; DEATH SHALL NO LONGER HAVE DOMINION OVER HIM.

Rom. 6:9

ALLELUIA

GOD OUR FATHER

WE ARE GATHERED HERE TO SHARE WHICH YOUR ONLY SON LEFT TO HIS CHURCH TO IN THE SUPPER HE GAVE IT TO US WHEN HE WAS ABOUT REVEAL HIS LOVE AND COMMANDED US TO CELEBRATE IT TO DIE AS THE NEW AND ETERNAL SACRIFICE

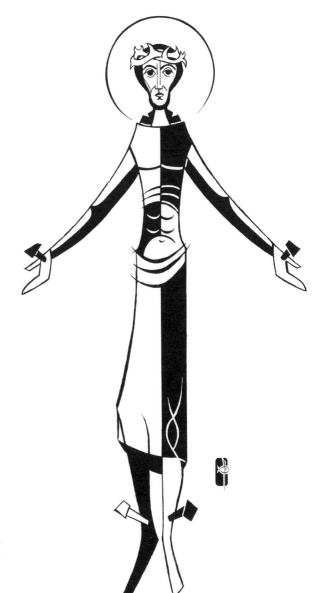

REJOICE THE ALLELUIA LORD is RISEN

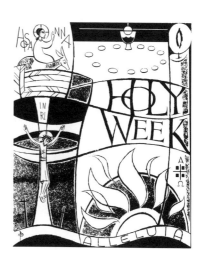

CHRIST

HAVING
RISEN FROM THE
DEAD, DIES
NOW NO MORE;
DEATH SHALL
NO LONGER
HAVE DOMIN-
ION OVER
HIM.
ROM. 6:9

ALLELUIA

THE LAMB HAS REDEEMED THE SHEEP ALLELUIA

REJOICE THE LORD

ALLELUIA

is RISEN

Alleluia! Alleluia!
sweet the wood,
sweet the load that hangs on you!
sweet the nails,

GOD OUR FATHER,

WE ARE GATHERED HERE TO SHARE IN THE SUPPER WHICH YOUR ONLY SON LEFT TO HIS CHURCH TO REVEAL HIS LOVE. HE GAVE IT TO US WHEN HE WAS ABOUT TO DIE AND COMMANDED US TO CELEBRATE IT AS THE NEW AND ETERNAL SACRIFICE.

HAS CHANGED OUR DARK NIGHT INTO SUNRISE

passiontide

alleluia! alleluia!

sweet the wood, sweet the nails,

sweet the load that hangs on you!

AROSE AND AM STILL WITH YOU

HOSANNA

CHRIST IS RISEN

BREAD OF LIFE • CUP OF ETERNAL SALVATION

WORSHIP
THANK
PRAISE
HIM

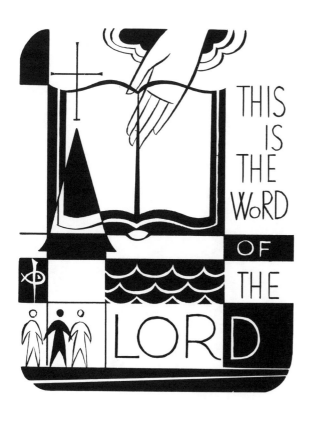

THIS
IS
THE
WORD
OF
THE
LORD

LET US
GIVE THANKS
TO THE
LORD OUR
GOD

Jesus then took the loaves of bread, gave thanks, and passed them around. —Today's Gospel

YOUR WORD IS A LAMP TO GUIDE MY STEPS.

PSALMS 118,105

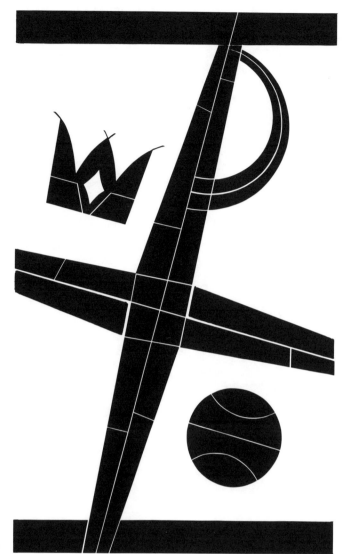

HOSANNA

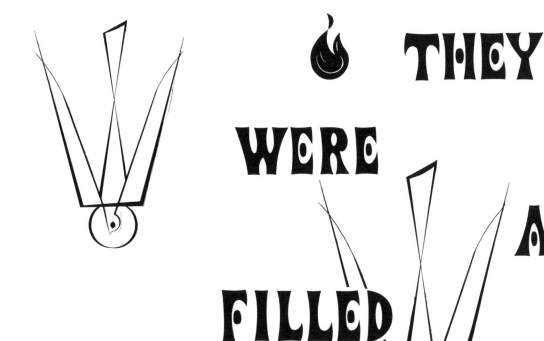

THEY

WERE

ALL

FILLED

WITH

THE

HOLY SPIRIT

THEY

WERE

ALL

FILLED

WITH

THE

HOLY SPIRIT

LORD SEND OUT YOUR SPIRIT AND RENEW THE FACE OF THE EARTH

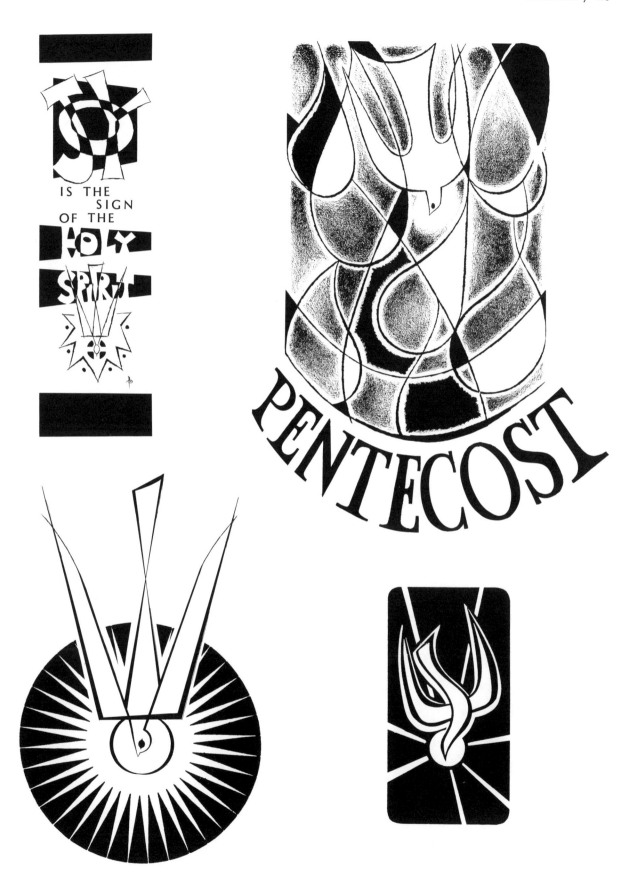

IS THE
SIGN
OF THE
HOLY
SPIRIT

PENTECOST

His Ascension is our glory and our hope

Glory be to the Father,

through the Son,

in the Holy Spirit !

BEHOLD THE HEART WHICH HAS LOVED MEN SO GREATLY BUT WHICH HAS BEEN GIVEN SO LITTLE LOVE IN RETURN

FEAST OF THE MOST SACRED HEART

FEAST OF THE MOST SACRED HEART

All honor   to you

MARY

MARY

TODAY THE VIRGIN **MARY** IS TAKEN UP TO HEAVEN Rejoice SHE REIGNS WITH CHRIST FOREVER

SHE REIGNS WITH CHRIST FOR EVER

TODAY THE VIRGIN **MARY** IS TAKEN UP TO HEAVEN LET US **Rejoice**

FEAST OF THE ASSUMPTION

TODAY THE VIRGIN **MARY** IS TAKEN UP TO HEAVEN **Rejoice** SHE REIGNS WITH CHRIST FOREVER

Sing praise to God all you his martyr saints

STS. SIMON and JUDE — Apostles

ST.
ELIZABETH
ANN SETON

SAINT MARGARET CLITHEROW

kept Lent well by her Passover
in Christ from death to life!

Happy are you, holy Virgin Mary, deserving of all praise;

from you rose the sun of justice, Christ the Lord. Alleluia Verse
—Birth of Mary

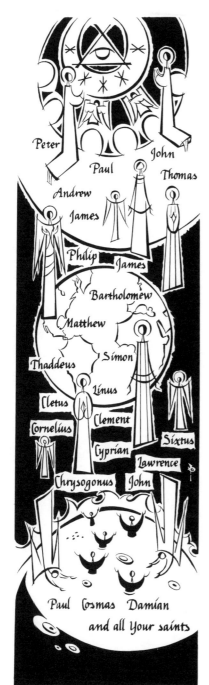

ALL YOU SAINTS BLESS THE LORD

Peter
Paul
John
Andrew
Thomas
James
Philip
James
Bartholomew
Matthew
Thaddeus
Simon
Cletus
Linus
Cornelius
Clement
Cyprian
Sixtus
Lawrence
Chrysogonus
John
Paul Cosmas Damian
and all Your saints

FEAST
OF THE
QUEENSHIP
OF
Mary

S. BENEDICT

HOLY
RULE

ST
CLOUD

ST. GREGORY the GREAT

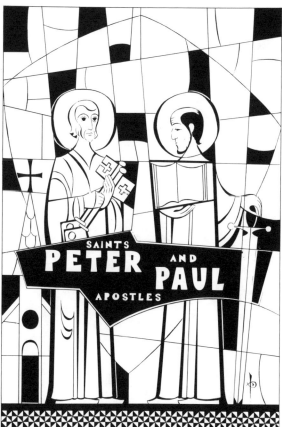

SAINTS
PETER AND PAUL
APOSTLES

ST THOMAS MORE

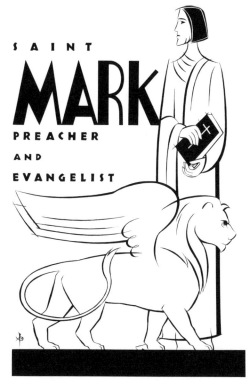

SAINT MARK
PREACHER
AND
EVANGELIST

ST. MATTHEW

the CON-VERSION of ST. PAUL

SAINT
DOMINIC

ST. JOSEPH THE WORKER

WELCOME
MATTHEW

YOU
ALONE
WERE
WORTHY
TO
BEAR THE
PRICE OF
THE WORLD'S RANSOM

WHO CONQUERED BY A TREE—

—ON A TREE WAS CONQUERED . . .

My soul is thirsting for you O Lord my God, as in a dry & weary land where no water is ...

The eyes of all look hopefully to you, and you give them their food in due season.

—Responsorial Psalm 145

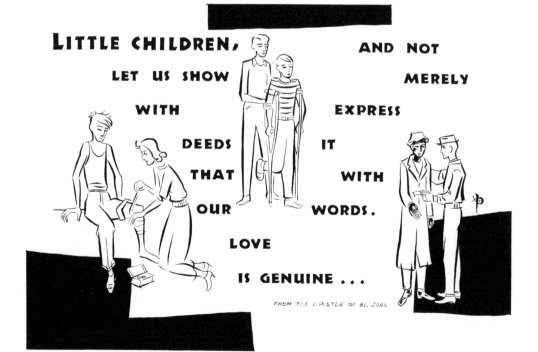

LITTLE CHILDREN, LET US SHOW WITH DEEDS THAT OUR LOVE IS GENUINE ... AND NOT MERELY EXPRESS IT WITH WORDS.

FROM THE EPISTLE OF BL. JOHN

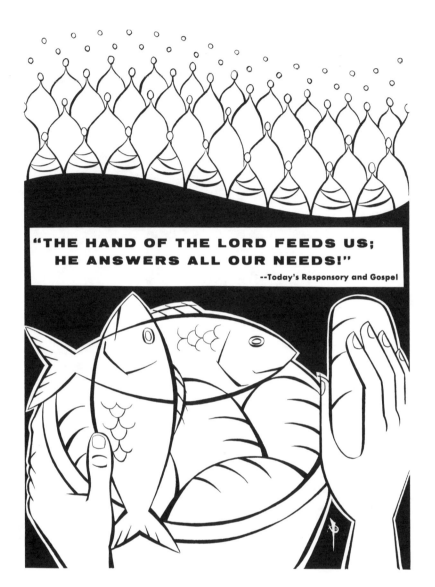

"THE HAND OF THE LORD FEEDS US;
HE ANSWERS ALL OUR NEEDS!"

--Today's Responsory and Gospel

GOD HAS GIVEN ME THE RICHES OF HIS GRACE

FAITH HOPE LOVE

I AM THE WAY, THE TRUTH AND THE LIFE

LET US GATHER TOGETHER TO ASK THE LORD'S BLESSING

A tree is known by its fruit.

"THIS IS GOD'S CHOSEN ONE."

I WILL SING
TO THE LORD
AS LONG AS I LIVE

I WILL SING
PRAISE TO MY GOD
WHILE I HAVE
MY   BEING

CHARITY

I REJOICED
BECAUSE THEY SAID TO ME WE WILL GO UP TO THE HOUSE OF THE LORD

GRADUAL

The eyes of all look hopefully to you, and you give them their food in due season.

—Responsorial Psalm 145

I AM THE LIVING BREAD WHICH HAS COME DOWN FROM HEAVEN. EXCEPT YOU EAT THE FLESH OF THE SON OF MAN AND DRINK HIS BLOOD YOU SHALL NOT HAVE LIFE IN YOU.

"THIS IS GOD'S CHOSEN ONE."

—Today's Gospel

*If I speak with human tongues and angelic as well,
but do not have love,
I am a noisy gong, a clanging cymbal.*

is patient,
is kind
is not jealous,
does not put on airs,
is not snobbish,
is never rude,
is not self-seeking,

is not prone to anger,
does not brood over injuries,
does not rejoice in what is wrong,
but rejoices with the truth. . . .
LOVE NEVER FAILS.
—1 Corinthians 13

A tree is known by its fruit.

LOVE

PEACE

FAITH

"MASTER, HOW GOOD IT IS FOR US TO BE HERE."

MOSES

JESUS

ELIJAH

"Come after me; I will make you fishers of my people."
—Today's Gospel

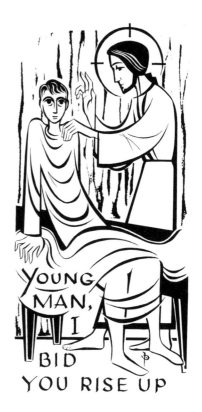

YOUNG MAN, I BID YOU RISE UP

LET US GATHER TOGETHER TO ASK THE LORD'S BLESSING

EVERY TREE THAT DOES NOT BEAR GOOD FRUIT IS CUT DOWN AND THROWN INTO THE FIRE.
—TODAY'S GOSPEL

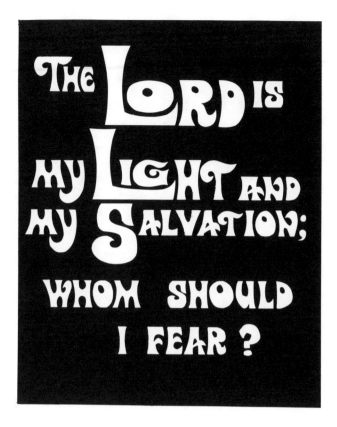

THE LORD IS MY LIGHT AND MY SALVATION; WHOM SHOULD I FEAR?

LORD YOU ARE MY ROCK AND FORTRESS

I REJOICED BECAUSE THEY SAID TO ME WE WILL GO UP TO THE HOUSE OF THE LORD

GRADUAL

EVERY TREE THAT DOES NOT BEAR GOOD FRUIT IS CUT DOWN AND THROWN INTO THE FIRE.

—TODAY'S GOSPEL

But for you who fear my name, there will arise the sun of justice with its healing rays.
—1st reading

"EVERYONE WHO EXALTS HIMSELF SHALL BE HUMBLED WHILE HE WHO HUMBLES HIMSELF SHALL BE EXALTED"
LUKE 18:9-14

"EVERYONE WHO EXALTS HIMSELF SHALL BE HUMBLED WHILE HE WHO HUMBLES HIMSELF SHALL BE EXALTED"
LUKE 18:9-14

"There is no chaining the word of God!"

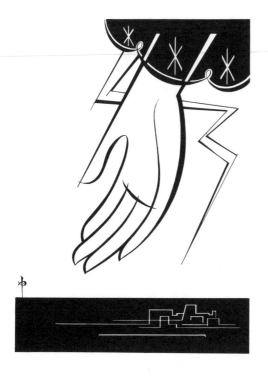

"**Go,**
therefore,
and make
disciples
of all the
nations.
Baptize
them in
the name
of the
Father, and
of the
Son,
and of
the
Holy
Spirit."

(Matthew
28:19)

—Today's Gospel

"**Go,**
therefore,
and make
disciples
of all the
nations.
Baptize
them in
the name
of the
Father, and
of the
Son,
and of
the
Holy
Spirit."

(Matthew
28:19)

—Today's Gospel

O God, let all the nations praise you!

O Jerusalem

HE WHO EATS
MY FLESH
ABIDES IN ME
AND I IN HIM

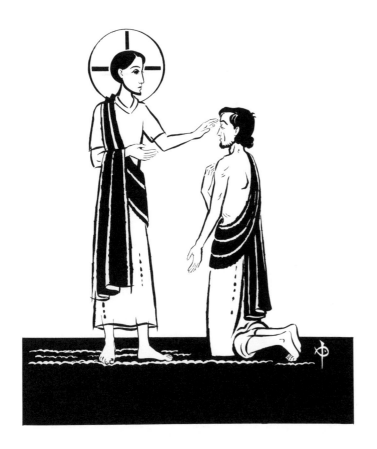

YOUNG MAN, I BID YOU RISE UP

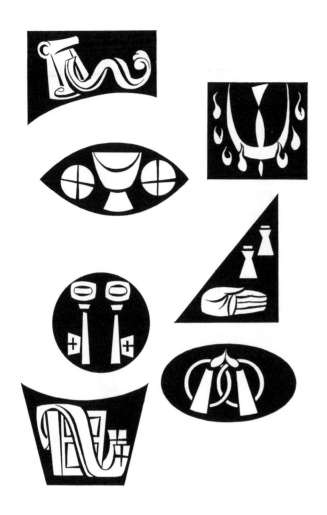

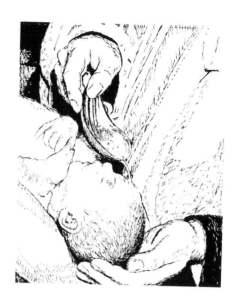

Body of Christ

MORNING PRAYER   **EVENING PRAYER**

IS THE
ECHO OF
GoD's
LiFe

WITHIN US

MARMION

HE HAS
FILLED
THE HUNGRY
WITH
GOOD THINGS

THOU
SAYEST IT:
I AM
A KING

LET US PRAY
FOR GOD'S
HOLY
CHURCH

HOLY
MOTHER
CHURCH

SPOUSE
OF
CHRIST

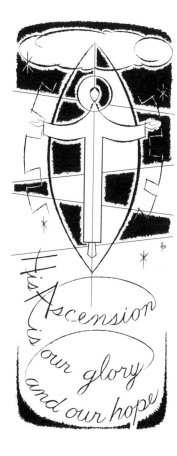

His Ascension is our glory and our hope

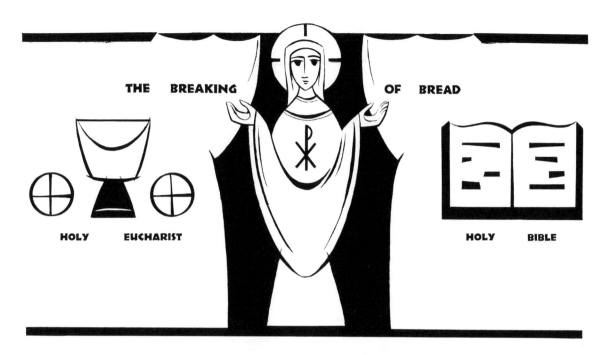

THE BREAKING OF BREAD

HOLY EUCHARIST

HOLY BIBLE

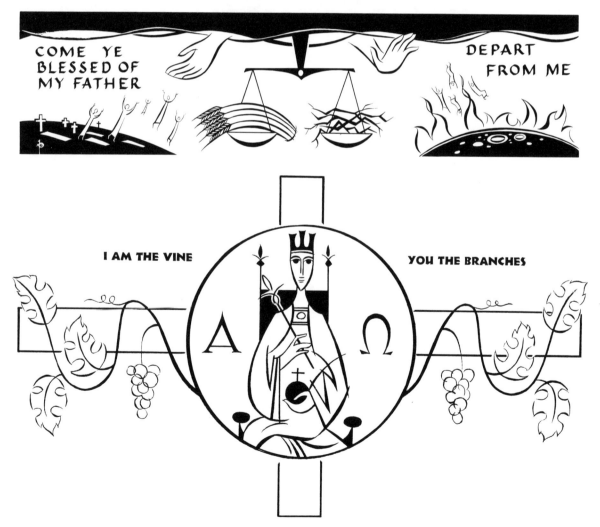

COME YE BLESSED OF MY FATHER

DEPART FROM ME

I AM THE VINE

YOU THE BRANCHES

FEB. 2 CANDLEMAS

EPIPHANY

Christmas

CHRIST'S COMING

SUNDAYS OF PENTECOST

PENTECOST

ASCENSION

Easter

PASSIONTIDE

LENT

ADAM

SEPTUAGESIMA

BLESSED ✠ ARE ...

THE POOR IN SPIRIT +

THE MEEK

THEY THAT MOURN

 THAT HUNGER

+

THE MERCIFUL

THE CLEAN OF HEART

THE PEACEMAKERS

THEY THAT SUFFER

"Come by yourselves
to an out-of-the-way place
and rest a little."

—Today's Gospel

℟. Lord, send out your Spirit,
and renew the face of the earth.

Bless the Lord, O my soul!
O Lord, my God, you are great indeed!
How manifold are your works, O Lord!
the earth is full of your creatures.

℟. Lord, send out your Spirit,
and renew the face of the earth.

If you take away their breath, they perish
and return to their dust.
When you send forth your spirit, they are
created,
and you renew the face of the earth.

℟. Lord, send out your Spirit,
and renew
the face of the earth.